BLACK GIRL UGLY

The Art of Approach and Engagement

WALTER ROBINSON, SR.

TESTIMONIALS

As a Black woman, I must admit that the title Black Girl Ugly initially gave me pause. However, once I began reading, I quickly realized that the story delves far deeper than its title suggests. The book resonated with me profoundly—particularly in its exploration of identity, self-worth, and resilience. As a mother of Black sons, I found many of its themes deeply relatable, prompting me to reflect on my own family values, parenting approaches, and expectations for my children. It also inspired me to reconsider my past relationships and the ways personal history shapes our understanding of love and belonging.

Black Girl Ugly is an insightful, thought-provoking, and emotionally honest work. It offers a mirror for self-reflection and a lens through which to better understand the experiences that shape us. I highly recommend this book to anyone seeking a powerful and relatable story about growth, healing, and self-discovery.

Dr. Kimberly Thomas-Smith
Psychologist/Author

- - - - -

In my nearly 30 years of working, or being affiliated, with the California Department of Corrections and Rehabilitation, when I read this book, my first instinctual thought was this needed to be added to the instructional toolkit for every man leaving prison. Incarcerated people who serve long prison terms, have many challenges, and the one that is not talked about, but can be a real impediment to a successful return to the community, is how to build or attract meaningful relationships with the opposite sex.

Just think, a guy that has been locked away for 5, 10, 15, or 20+ years, has not had much practice in engaging the opposite sex seeking romantic or intersex relationships. How do you get through the rust, without instruction? I've seen and I know a lot of lonely men who are successful in many ways, except with the opposite sex. This book will fix that for most once it is in their hands.

Additionally, the other side of the carceral system are the employees who work in prisons, who have higher than usual societal divorce rates. Just like the formerly incarcerated, these employees are off the market for years, and are returning to the dating game as novice. They may have been skilled beforehand in their dating/mating approach; but if you don't use those skills, it isn't like riding a bike. Black Girl Ugly is the prescription for helping them get to, or return to, top form.

Samuel R.
Retired Captain (A)
Former Public Information Officer
San Quentin State Prison

- - - - -

I always felt a bit awkward sitting inside barbershops, even though I was there for valid reasons. I'd sit as my boys got their haircuts, but always felt like I was eavesdropping on conversations not meant for my ears.

This book felt similar. A peek into the interior world of Black men, unfiltered and unperformed. It's the quiet vulnerability behind the bravado, the truth that hides between jokes and nods.

Black Girl Ugly lets you witness what happens when men remember their softness, when they confront the ugly and come out honest.

For me, it wasn't just reading. It was listening. Listening to the kind of truths women rarely get to hear and men rarely get to say.

**Mya James
RevOps Leader/Public Speaker/Author**

BLACK GIRL UGLY

The Art of Approach and Engagement

Black Girl Ugly: The Art of Approach and Engagement
Written by: Walter Robinson, Sr.

Copyright © 2026 by Walter Robinson, Sr..
All rights reserved.
Published in the United States of America.

No part of this publication may be reproduced, stored, or transmitted in any form or by any means, electronic, mechanical, photocopying, recording, scanning, or otherwise, without written permission from the publisher. It is illegal to copy this book, post it to a website, or distribute it by any other means without permission except in the case of brief quotations embodied in critical articles and reviews, or as permitted by US copyright law. For information, write to 4505 Montara Dr., Antioch, CA 94531.

Revision Publishing LLC books may be purchased for educational, business, or sales promotional use. For information, please email contact@revisionpub.com or visit www.revisionpub.com.

First edition

Library of Congress Control Number: 2025923149
Robinson Sr., Walter. Black Girl Ugly: The Art of Approach and Engagement / Walter Robinson Sr. - 1.) SEL023000 - SELF-HELP / Personal Growth / Self-Esteem 2.) FAM051000 - FAMILY & RELATIONSHIPS / Dating 3.) FAM029000 - FAMILY & RELATIONSHIPS / Love & Romance.

ISBN 979-8-9936608-1-3 (hardcover)
ISBN 979-8-9936608-0-6 (paperback)
ISBN 979-8-9936608-2-0 (eBook)

Editing by Chanekka Pullens
Cover/Interior Design by Hot Book Covers

I would like to dedicate this book to my daughters and sons, in hopes that the energy of this book finds my sons' and my daughters' future mates.

NOTE OF TERMINOLOGY AND USAGE

I know the name of the book brings up various emotions, and initially led to some controversial conversations. When I decided on "Black Girl Ugly" as the name of this book, it was in no way meant to demean, disgrace, or put Black women down in any way. I chose to use the name "Black Girl Ugly" because after a total of 24 years of being in two relationships that led to two marriages, and eventually two divorces, at the age of 46, I found myself back in the dating pool, and I couldn't find a way to connect with Black women. After two months of continued rejections, I started to refer to myself as being Black girl ugly to my friends and family. I truly felt like Black women did not find me attractive at all anymore. I have always dated Black women and never really had an eye for any other race; it was just during this time in my life I felt like the women of my race didn't have an eye for me.

So why should you read such a sad story? I don't believe you should read such a sad story. This book does begin with that narrative but definitely doesn't end there. I had a chance encounter at a club that changed everything for me, and now I am talking to Black women with an 85% success rate. As you read through these pages, I am confident that you too will find a similar success rate that I have had with approaching and engaging women. I wrote this book to meet you where you are today and give you the tools to successfully talk to the woman you desire.

TABLE OF CONTENTS

Introduction — 15

Chapter 1: The Golden Dragon — 23

Chapter 2: The Lab — 37

Chapter 3: The Approach. — 49
    Exercise #1: Good Morning, I'm Doing This For Me
    Exercise #2: Check Your Energy Level
    Exercise #3: Check Your Posture
    Exercise #4: Hold Eye Contact

Chapter 4: The Engagement — 69
    Exercise #5: Building a Web
    Exercise #6: Conversation Zones
    Exercise #7: Pivot Questions

Chapter 5: The Close — 95
    Exercise # 8: The Offer/Close

INTRODUCTION

It was 2021, and for many, the harsh effects of the pandemic felt like it was finally behind them. We could breathe fresh air again, those masks that had become an essential part of our life eventually started coming off in public. We could actually see one another's face, and many were returning to the office for work. We were again dining in restaurants; some brave souls had even returned to bars, nightclubs, and gyms. We all yearned for the connection that had been lost during two years of sheltering in place.

2021 was a year when the world was striving to regain a sense of normalcy. Yet, for some people, 2021 was a year of trying to pick up the pieces from the losses they had experienced from COVID-19. The pandemic had killed over 5,000,000 people, leaving many scattered with their emotions and grief. It left many trying to figure out ways to process the trauma of losing multiple relatives and significant others in a matter of days, weeks, and months. I vividly remember my friends sharing stories of how they had to say their last goodbyes via an iPad. They were not able to be there for their loved ones and, in some cases, families were not able to give their loved ones a proper funeral or farewell. There was so much to recover from in the years that COVID-19 wreaked havoc on this world — physically, emotionally, and spiritually.

During the pandemic, COVID-19 not only damaged people's health and mental well-being; it also struck hard in another area — relationships. Many couples couldn't survive the stress of going through the pandemic together. For some, trying to find connections after the trauma of sudden loss was too difficult. For others, being confined at home with their partner for long periods of time drew them

INTRODUCTION

further away instead of closer together. I believe that because we were locked away from society for so long, once civilization was able to come back together, many people yearned for new or different connections. That longing, that curiosity for something unfamiliar, led some to struggle with the temptation of infidelity. I happen to be a COVID-19 relationship casualty.

Now, in 2021, I ended my 15-year quote unquote marriage. This was my second marriage; my first marriage lasted five years, and we dated for four years before getting married. On the day that marriage was officially dissolved, I met my second wife. With no therapy, no healing, no understanding of really what went wrong in the first marriage, eight months later, I would be standing at the altar once again, saying "I do" — this time to wife number two. Now like I said earlier, 15 years later, I would be ending that relationship as well. I said quote unquote for a reason, but I will not reveal which of the previous COVID-19 obstacles ended my relationship in this book; let's just say the end of my marriage is now a case study. I know I have piqued your interest about what happened, but you will have to wait for the presumably forthcoming book tour to get that answer — because that's not what this book is about. I guess I am just making sure I will get to answer at least one question during the question-and-answer portion of the tour. Anyway, I'm single again, and I can honestly say I've spent my entire adulthood in relationships. I never dated in high school. Really, the only two women I tried to talk to and had some success with were the only two relationships I had, and they both ended in divorce.

Now, at the time of my newfound singleness, I have a successful career, own a business, and enjoy a stable lifestyle. At 46, I found myself desiring feminine companionship.

Let me be 100 — when I started looking for connection, I was intentionally trying to connect with Black women. Just for clarity, before I even jumped back into the dating pool, I had spent seven months in therapy. My therapist and I had discussed the kind of women I had a propensity to date — which, honestly,

INTRODUCTION

wasn't good for me at all — and what I should be looking for in a new companion.

After all the inner work I had been doing, I truly felt ready to get back out there. So, when I decided to finally jump into the dating pool, I made a full-blown effort — I'd try to make eye contact, offer a smile, or just say hello. But it would all end up the same way. Some would turn their heads as I approached. Others would drop their heads so I couldn't make eye contact. Sadly, this happened most often when I tried to approach and talk to Black women. Women of other races would embrace or accept at least some of the advancements, but when it came to the ones I really wanted to engage with, I was at a total loss. After months of failed attempts to talk and engage with my Black women, I came up with the term that I have titled this book, "Black Girl Ugly".

I had to be Black girl ugly because every other race would show me attention or even somewhat acknowledge the bid to flirt or connect. Still, I was striking out 100 percent of the time when it came to the Black queens. To be honest, I don't even think I was striking out; I don't believe I was even being let on the field.

I am writing this book because that's where my journey began. I went from being *Black girl ugly* to stepping onto the field as a starter — with a success rate of about 85-90% when it came to approaching, engaging, and pursuing women.

Before you dive deeper into the book, you probably want to know the type of woman I like to pursue. When it came to my pursuit of women, my professional preferences were all over the place. I can honestly say the women I was drawn to were accomplished in their own right — nurses, lawyers, doctors, models, therapists, life coaches, even women serving in the military. I do have a physical type, but I would rather not attempt to objectify women by their looks.

So, now I'm writing this book for the men that are walking around like I once was — thinking they are *Black girl ugly* or simply

INTRODUCTION

feeling unattractive to women in general. This book is not about how to attract or obtain one race of women. The information and tools within these pages are designed to prepare and set you up to have success in approaching and engaging women of any nationality or culture you desire to connect with. No longer do you have to feel like everyone is out of your league or that you don't stand a chance with her. You're about to crack the code — the art of approach and engagement — in the pursuit of your life partner.

CHAPTER ONE
THE GOLDEN DRAGON

It was a Friday night in April, and I think my cousin was tired of me sitting around, complaining and contemplating ways to get back with my ex. At this time, I figured that was the only Black woman that I probably had a chance at getting. So, my cousin called me up, and said, "We are going out tonight — and don't dress like a husband or father, so no dress/casual shoes or relaxed-fit jeans."

That meant I had to rush to a department store to find an outfit for the night. By the time he got to my house, I was straight. I'd already had two Moscow mules to loosen up, and my clothes were on point. I went from relaxed-fit jeans to an athletic, straight-fit pair, and I traded in my dress shoes for a pair of white and baby blue retro Nike Air Max. You know, I was feeling myself. My cousin doesn't tell me where we're going, but we end up at the Golden Dragon.

The Golden Dragon is a Chinese restaurant that converts to a club at night. Now, I don't know why it was here at this specific place where things began to change for me. The Golden Dragon of all places.

When I started working on this book, the Golden Dragon was the first thing I researched. I found out that the Golden Dragon represents wisdom, wealth, and spiritual growth across various cultures and spiritual practices. It is often said to have emerged from primordial chaos, bringing order to the universe — a symbol of transformation and creation, reflecting the cycle of life.

It is also believed that having a strong connection with the dragon leads to the development of inner strength and self-discovery. The Golden Dragon doesn't hoard its

CHAPTER ONE: THE GOLDEN DRAGON

treasures, unlike the dragons of myth. Instead, it is known to share its riches, bringing prosperity to those who are worthy and pure of heart. This symbolizes the spiritual principle that true wealth and prosperity come from sharing and generosity. After learning this, it made sense that it was here where my breakthrough had to happen.

Now, the night starts off as usual for me. I would look at the Black women, and they drop or turn their heads. When I would look at every other race of ladies, they were smiling back — some even offer light conversation. But I tell you, I am feeling myself that night and adding to my drink count quickly. So, I'm talking to my cousin and confirming that I really have to be Black girl ugly because now he got a chance to see with his own eyes what's happening to me. For him, he is either trying to encourage me or not buying it; however, he is just letting me talk. Eventually, I go to the bar to get another drink, and an Asian girl comes up. She asks what I'm drinking and offers to buy me a drink. I'm asking myself, "Why won't any of these Black women here give me that attention?" I go back to the wall where my cousin is, and this fine, brown-skinned woman walks by, smiling at me as she passes. When I say she was fine, this sister was all that: pretty face, small waist, and the assets were asseting (**her figure was well put together*). Okay, it was different for me, a sister actually looked my way; but there was one key problem, she came with a dude in tow.

As the night went on, I decided to stand at the bar and mingle with those who wanted to mingle. And guess who found themselves within arm's reach of me? *Ms. Fine.* This time, she was not with the dude — she was talking to some chick. Now to be honest, it has never been my style to talk to a lady when I know they are with someone, especially at a bar or club with a lot of drinking going on. That night was no different. However, she was only an arm's length from me. Even though I caught another smile from her, I still wasn't going to pursue her. The night was going too well to get a fo' sho turn down (in my mind).

CHAPTER ONE: THE GOLDEN DRAGON

But then the ancestors stepped in. She started taking off her jacket, and her arm was stretched right in front of me. It was my gentleman's reaction to help her get her jacket off. She took my hand, and said, "Thank you. Now you have to dance with me."

Next thing I know, she's leading me to the dance floor, and we danced most of the night. I was so glad my 6'3, 325-pound cousin was there because it limited any confrontation from happening. As the night was ending, my cousin said, "Let's go." I finished my 10th or 11th drink that night and began walking to the car.

Just as I was getting in the car, *Ms. Fine* came around the corner and said, "What's Up! You're not going to give a name with a number attached to it?"

I was like, "Didn't you come here with *dude?*"

Her reply was, "I'm out here trying to

talk to you, don't worry about him."

Now, in my mind, I'm thinking, *my cousin was right; I guess clothes do attract.* But remember, I'm ten drinks in, so what came out of my mouth was, "For real? You out here trying to talk to me? Why are you doing that, because I thought I was *Black girl ugly!*"

You should have seen my cousin's face; he could have dropped-kicked me on the spot.

She responded, "WHAT? WHERE DID YOU GET THAT NONSENSE FROM! Give me your number, I will give you mine, and we will talk by tomorrow night."

This woman was direct. She knew what she wanted. And it was in our future conversations that gave me the initial understanding of how to pursue Black women, well, let me just say any woman successfully.

Going back to the lore of the Golden Dragon. The dragon leads to the development of inner strength and wisdom, and it was her and some other Black women that did just that for me. When I said she was fine, she was stripper fine, because weeks later, I found out that was her occupation. We talked for about two months, nothing too serious, more so as friends. You have to remember that when you're getting out of a marriage, any relationship or a situation is not going to last long. You're carrying and discussing all your hurt, and nobody has time to be your unpaid therapist.

We hung out about twice, but I remember the first time we did, she was like, "Walt, I was a little nervous about what you were going to actually look like because of your *Black girl ugly* comment." She said, "I was like, I wonder if I was drinking too much, and I drank looks on you that night. Now that I see you, you are far from ugly."

My response was, "If I am not *Black girl ugly (still believing the story I created and the lie within me)*, why can't I even get a Black woman to look at me? Every time I try to make eye contact, they just drop their heads or look away."

Her response is what I identify as **Lesson #1 - Have Confidence.** She said, "Walt, Black women are attracted to confidence. Not necessarily arrogance or cockiness but having a sure confidence of who you are and what you represent. No one has time to build a man's confidence. So he can find some newfound energy and cheat on you after you have helped give him the basics? He at least has to come stepping to us with the basics, and we can sniff out a lack of confidence even before you approach." She went on, " I can tell from our conversations your confidence and self-esteem is low because when you talk about yourself, you only talk about what you do and what you have."

Now I couldn't let her just say that with me not defending myself. I had to rebut and try to ward off this verbal attack, but she was right. I had no confidence, especially when it came to approaching and talking to the ladies. I kept my chin down, energy low, and my huge,

CHAPTER ONE: THE GOLDEN DRAGON

broad shoulders slumped, and that was the first impression I was giving before any type of approach.

So, a little about me. I grew up in an era when being light-skinned and thin was in, and I was never neither. I used to be 5'9, age does shrink you. But I'm a 5'8 dark chocolate man that has a body that has always packed a punch or a lunch, or however you say it.

Let's get into a little story time. I remember one moment in 7th grade. There was this girl who, I believe, was trying to be nice, I guess. You remember back in the day when you would get your school pictures back and trade them with your friends? Well, she asked for one of mine.

A couple of days later, we were in class, and she told me probably one of the most hurtful things a little seventh grader could hear: "My mom told me to give you your picture back because you are not cute at all."

Now, you have to remember — I had just started junior high school, back in my day, we left elementary school in 6th grade. So, 7th grade was the year that you really start identifying your likes and urges to connect with the opposite sex. Just for clarity, this is not a girl I had any interest in or any desire for, she was like a cool friend. But what I heard her mom say in my head was, "Go take that picture back; that little boy is ugly as hell." And I remember thinking, *Wow, Mom, why did you have to be so harsh?*

Now don't worry, I am giggling as I write this, and I'm definitely not holding on to it in a painful way. For the record, her daughter later tried to talk to me when we were adults. In my mind, she only wanted to talk to me because I was well established at the time, (*Ms. Fine* was right, dang it), but I can't lie — her mom's words did have some effect on me for a while.

There was another occasion when the phone dating line was a way to connect. I was talking to this sister, and we decided to meet up. She and her friends rolled up on me at my

CHAPTER ONE: THE GOLDEN DRAGON

house, saw me, and said, "Oh hell Naw!!!" Then drove away. Even though these experiences happened way before my two marriages, I remember walking away from both moments pretty much deflated, like maybe God kept me out of the looks pool. Experiences like those helped shape the lack of confidence I had when it came to connecting with the ladies. Not to mention, I was the husky brother of four Slim Jims growing up. So yeah, *Ms. Fine* was right. I didn't know what true confidence looked like, let alone what it felt like.

I didn't know what it looked like or even what it was, but it was going to be my mission to try to find it, especially if I was going to have any hope of getting the woman I was interested in pursuing. I hope you understand that I have a type when it comes to dating, and I knew I wouldn't even have the opportunity to engage with my type unless I changed some things about myself. Let's go back to the Golden Dragon. It is believed by many cultures that the Golden Dragon symbolizes self-discovery. If I were to date that successfully stable businesswoman

I truly wanted to be with and have a healthy relationship with her, I would have to sit with myself and discover who I really am.

Confidence appears differently and manifests differently for each person. I can't give you the magic pill to suddenly obtain it, but I can provide you with insight on how to get there. True self-confidence comes from an honest self-examination of who you are. First, when you hear you lack confidence, I don't care what your financial or social status is, don't immediately take offence. Just sit with it and explore it, because a healthier you may be on the other side of your exploration. You must also come to an understanding of the lies you are accepting and believing about yourself. I know this is going to sound cliché, but you have to rip off the old to become the new.

I wrote about these two incidents from my youth — about being told and being made to feel unattractive for a reason. It was those and countless other experiences I had that made me form my opinion, or rather, the lie in my mind that I was unattractive. If that is my belief, how do I overcome that? No matter how many family members or friends tell you the opposite, you seem to always believe the very few that got you to buy into the lie in the first place. Now you are faced with — if looks are part of the first impression and you feel like you are heavily lacking in that area, how do you build confidence in a way that is attractive enough to at least get the first eye contact?

Let's go back to our friend the dragon. You must take the time to rediscover who you are and self-discover what and how you desire to present yourself to the world. This will give you confidence and clarity to bring out the best in yourself daily. With the tools you will find in this book, the fear and frustration we all get when we want to approach will be minimal to none. So, let's talk about some tools to create your plan for success.

CHAPTER TWO
THE LAB

If I was going to work on myself and get some real answers, I was going to have to go to my lab. Everyone needs a lab. The lab is your circle of accountability and exploration. It is in that lab where you can truly get out of your own head. You should have someone in your lab who keeps you accountable, not in a mean, jealous, or arrogant way, but in a way that allows you to feel free to talk. They will do their best to guide you in the right direction. To tell you the truth, you may need more than one of these types of people in your lab. You also need a thought exploration person in your lab. This person is the one who is going to listen, not judge, but provide you with nuggets to help you further develop your thoughts and opinions. Now, for me, this person was my therapist. Back then, I saw my therapist every week. I probably should have seen her twice a week. Nonetheless, it's every other week now.

Now after my conversation with *Ms. Fine*, I couldn't wait until my Tuesday appointment to return to the lab and discuss these new findings. When I logged on for my appointment, she could barely get the standard, "How are you feeling?" She knew my belief that I felt I was *Black girl ugly*. She knew it was tearing down the little confidence I had even further, and on this day, I had identified the problem, and I needed a quick fix to solve it.

Here's how me and my therapist conversation went down:

Me: So, I went out with *Ms. Fine* last week. It was cool, but she gave me the reason why I am *Black girl ugly*.

Therapist: What is that?

Me: It's my confidence. I have no confidence in myself when it comes to women.

Therapist: Do you believe that to be true?

Me: I think she is on to something.

Therapist: Why is that?

Me: Because of some of the body image and colorism issues I dealt with in my youth, and even some in my adulthood.

Therapist: Well, let's explore this.

    So, it certainly wasn't a quick fix. Probably over the next eight or nine sessions, we explored this topic in depth. I believe it was during our ninth session when she said something that I now call **Lesson #2** — what I consider a foundational step in building confidence. She said, "Walter, you have to understand that **OTHER PEOPLE'S PREFERENCE DOESN'T DETERMINE YOUR WORTH.**" That hit me like a ton of self-help books. We go throughout life basing our worth on what other people's preferences are toward us. But not only that, we define who we are and our value to this world based on the opinions of probably less than fifty people.

This idea was solidified for me as I thought about watching my children grow up. I was a park dad. I didn't mind taking my children to the park to play and interact with other kids, that's probably because I grew up shy and quiet. I felt like I missed out on a lot of opportunities because of it, and I didn't want them to have the same stumbling blocks that I did. Therefore, I made sure to foster their growth in social environments. When they were all around the age of three to six, making friends came so easily for them all. Here is an example of their exchanges:

My children: Hey, you want to play?

Kid: Play what?

CHAPTER TWO: THE LAB

My children: I don't know, we can make up a game.

Kid: Sure.

And the children would be off and playing most of the time until the park lights came on. However, between the ages of six and eight, things began to change. They were not as quick to approach a new kid with their freedom to engage. I would notice them playing by themselves for longer periods of time. They would scope around to see who would make eye contact or a friendly gesture before they would begin to approach and engage. It wasn't until recently that I actually put thought behind my own children's actions. From being outgoing extroverts who made every kid their best friend in a matter of five minutes, to being very careful of who and how they approached another child, they almost instantly morphed over the course of one to two years.

What happened between the ages of three and six? There were protected social and communal connections. Even though my children attended childcare, those were the same kids they were being raised with — the ones they learned to talk to, play with, and grow alongside. The childcare system provides a certain level of safe communal surroundings, but everyone in the community had to be open to befriending one another even if they didn't always get along. Because they were in the same place, they would eventually find some commonality and play with one another, so the only barrier they had was the lack of commonality. In their minds, if we are in the same place doing the same thing, then it's a no-brainer: this person is going to be my friend. The question now is what happens between the ages of six and eight?

Between the ages of six and eight, children start first and second grade. It is during these years that they first begin to find their independence in building their own community. They are building their community based on attitude, culture, likability, looks, among many other factors. However, it's not just my children building out their communities; other children are building their communities as well. It is in this space and time that they are hit with a harsh reality, and it's a reality that we often struggle to adapt to as adults as well. Primarily, childcare and preschool offer a protective, extended family-like environment. Therefore, because the environment was so protective and loving, the children had no fear or negative thoughts when it came to making new connections. How could they when every previous connection had been successful?

In the first grade they have found this new ability to choose their own connections and community. They go into it believing they are in total control about who they are going to add to their circle, and then all of a sudden, someone they thought fit in their group decides they don't want to be in their friend group. That's when they experience their first taste of relational rejection. There is another experience that hit my children very hard, too. That's when another child simply doesn't like them, and for whatever reason, they can't get along. So they distance themselves and their group from my child. Unlike childcare, where they were pretty much forced to get along and not feel the abandonment of relationships.

In first and second grade, they are faced with a new reality that life will continually challenge them with. How do I navigate my friendships? Who should be my friends, and who shouldn't be my friends? Who's okay to approach and who isn't? Does this sound familiar? Does it sound like your current outlook on dating or just engaging others as an adult? Before I get back to us adults, let's stay with the six- to eight-year-olds for a moment.

When the realization hits that they don't have total control over who they want in their friend group, and even worse, some people just don't want them as a friend, they start making mental notes and thoughts about who their ideal friends are. They go to their inner mental lab and start to build out what a friend is. What characteristics do they possess? What mannerisms do they show? Even at that age, they start looking at, how do they look?

CHAPTER TWO: THE LAB

Do they appear to be friendly? Do they look mischievous? Do they seem willing to include me, or will they separate me from their other friends? If you notice when they are at the park, they are looking and seeking answers to the same questions we are asking ourselves as adults.

Going back to the Golden Dragon, the dragon serves as a spiritual beacon of protection capable of imbuing one's life with stability, safety, and the courage to face challenges. As young children, they set out to build safety, stability, and protection around themselves. So that when they go to the park at ages six through eight, it becomes a whole different experience than the times they went at ages three and five.

When children reach the ages of six to eight, something changes. When they go to the park, they no longer run up to the first kid they see and ask, "Do you want to play?" Now they watch the kid and see what they are playing and who they are playing with. They are looking to see if they are nice and pleasant, or if they are finding trouble to get into. They are trying to determine if they can establish a connection with the child and what that connection would be. Finally, maintaining eye contact so they can ensure a positive experience. This sounds like trying to approach someone you want to talk to, doesn't it? I will answer that for the majority of you: "YES!" It's a yes because we are products of our childhood, our protections, our safeties, and, to be honest, some of our relational traumas, which we bring into our adulthood.

If you understand the scenario I just presented, you can see how many of our values — and even our sense of who we believe we are — are shaped by other people's preferences. We spend the majority of our time trying to fit others' preferences for acceptance, rather than doing the work and spending the time defining who we are. There is a powerful and impactful scene in this children's movie featuring lions. In this particular scene, the monkey goes to the young lion and asks him, "Who are you?" The young lion gave him his name. The monkey replied, "No, no, who are you?" Eventually, the monkey took him to the water where he was able to look in the water and see himself within. So let me guide you to the water.

That six- to eight-year-old kid is still here. They emerge every time there is an opportunity to establish a relational connection. They remind you of how some of those attempts to make connections in the past didn't work out for you. That young child within will always nudge you with your previous experiences and lessons from your youth, cautioning you to remember how to build strong relationships. Well, let's be honest, a lot of what little man reminds you to do is on point and should be taken into consideration. The part I want to focus on, though — and where he might lead you into error — is his idea to wait, watch, and welcome.

If you are waiting and watching, you may never get the opportunity to welcome. How many times have you waited and watched, and someone else walked right in with the corniest line and grabbed the girl's time and attention?

And now you are sitting there like, dang, I should have approached. I am not going to lie, I know I have been that person.

As we get ready to go and start developing your tools and skills to become a master at approaching and engaging women, you are going to always have to remind that little man in your head that it's best for you not to watch and wait. Now you have the tools in your toolbox to fix that issue that was so frightening for him in his day. Let's start developing and picking up the tools you will need to become skillful in the pursuit.

CHAPTER THREE
THE APPROACH

In this chapter, I aim to start addressing the approach. How do you confidently approach a Black woman — or any woman in general? How can you approach a woman with such confidence and success that your only concern is whether the two of you can actually connect and communicate? I know the approach can feel like the most difficult, heart-reckoning thing to do. This chapter will give you insight into how to approach someone — the easy part. Before we get there, let's dive back into the inner you. Let's return to our dragon friend. There is a belief in the dragon's ability to transform and create, symbolizing the cycle of life.

If we go back to the six- to eight-year-old version of you, there's probably a young kid trying to understand friendships — wondering why some people want to be your friend while others want nothing to do with you. With this newfound understanding that not everyone is going to like you, you likely had one of two reactions.

Reaction 1: You spent a lot of time trying to figure out why they didn't like you or want to be your friend.

Reaction 2: You took the approach that anyone who doesn't want to be your friend, that was their loss; too bad for them. I am embracing those who want to embrace me.

If you fall under **Reaction 1**, it's likely that you've adopted a life approach where most of your relational time is spent trying to fit into other people's preferences — molding yourself for their benefit rather than taking the time to develop and grow on your own. How many times have you left your healthy support system to chase the empty validation of another? Here

CHAPTER THREE: THE APPROACH

is a Bible reference for you.

In Luke 15:4-7, when Jesus uses the parable of the shepherd leaving the 99 to go after the one, you must be very clear and careful not to take it out of context. He was referring to a shepherd, and that was the shepherd's job to gather and protect the sheep. Let me be clear and reiterate, it is not your job to live up to the validation and preferences of others. Nor is it your job to conform to their opinions and thoughts about who you are and what you should be. This thought and mindset has hindered your confidence because you are carrying other people's mindsets and opinions about you. It is shaping how you move in this world on a day-to-day basis. Let's explore this even further.

What drives and motivates you? Could it be that you're aiming to prove people wrong or demonstrate your value? How about having the mindset that you know when you're done — people are going to have to praise and respect you? That all sounds like great reasons to strive to be better, doesn't it? I know it does because this used to be my own thinking. But you know who was missing out in these motivation equations? Me! I was never motivated to make a better me, for me. It always had to be an external factor to get me to strive for better.

What I realized is that even though I was striving and making great achievements in the process, my confidence and self-esteem were so low, I didn't feel worthy enough to do it for myself. You will never be able to continually and successfully approach and engage a possible mate until you understand and see the value within you. These are the main reasons I created the exercises in this book and chose to share them with you. Each one is designed to help you build confidence and make your interactions feel less stressful and more natural.

Exercise #1 GOOD MORNING:

I'M DOING THIS FOR ME

This is our first exercise. The exercises that we will go through in this book will help give

CHAPTER THREE: THE APPROACH

you confidence and the tools to be comfortable with your approach and engagements. We will start with what I call a warm-up. For at least the next two weeks, in passing, I want you to tell 5-10 strangers (preferably all female), "Good morning." "Good afternoon." Or, "Good evening." Now this is why I call it the I'm doing this for me exercise. After reading the last couple of paragraphs, some of you may have recognized that you have been living the majority of your life for others. Trying to get acceptance from others, trying to impress others, even your accountability has not been being accountable to yourself, but to others. This exercise, when you start, will be entirely for you, and you won't think or care about the response you get in the beginning.

You will quickly see the confidence you build when you know you're doing it solely for your enjoyment. You are probably saying, "Wait, Walt, did you say enjoyment? I'm going to get enjoyment by walking up and talking to complete strangers?" Believe me, YES! You are going to get enjoyment from talking to complete strangers.

Here is why:

1. You are stepping out and doing it for yourself. No one is forcing you, and you are going to see how quickly you become comfortable doing it.

2. You will see the positive responses you will get from others, just from having human interaction.

3. You will find your tone and energy to master your style to have successful approaches. It's in this exercise where it all starts.

Once you start during this exercise, you will definitely get enjoyment from seeing the reactions of the women you are speaking with once you find your right engagement energy.

Okay, now when you're ready to try **exercise #1**, remember to do it only when you are ready because you are doing it for you and nobody else including me. This is how I want you to do it. I don't want you to pass a person and just say, "Good morning." I want you to

CHAPTER THREE: THE APPROACH

walk with big energy, with the most upbeat attitude you can muster up on that day and give them a, "Hey, good morning!" The more upbeat the energy, the better. What you're going to find in a lot of cases is reciprocity. The recipient of your energy will try to bring that same energy back to you. You can play around with your energy and positivity levels to find that perfect tone and presence to receive the response and energy you would like to receive back.

Believe me, when you get your energy, tone, and positivity right, some women will even want to slow you down or stop you to engage in a conversation. This exercise will begin to break down the most difficult barrier of the approach — that being the first verbal communication. Now because you are doing this regularly and consistently, you are building up confidence and destroying that six- to eight-year-old kid who lost confidence in whether they should or shouldn't approach someone. You will quickly understand most people are yearning for a genuine and real connection, and maybe like you, are hesitant because that six- to eight-year-old kid inside of them doesn't want to get let down anymore.

I haven't forgotten about **Reaction #2**. Your group felt like you had more secure relationships. You've ensured yourself that only those who wanted to be in your space were allowed in, while those who were hesitant or didn't want to be there were kept out. Growing up, that way was a very safe and comfortable environment to be in. You pretty much had control of your whole environment. You mastered the six- to eight-year-old years. Building long-lasting and close friendships is something you definitely had down pat. But what many of you lack — and why you're probably reading this book about making connections in the dating world is this: when it comes to the entire dating scene, from approaching someone to being in a relationship, it requires vulnerability.

As a child, you pretty much gave up vulnerability for your protection. Now, for you, I need you to go into exercise one knowing that the approach is not an investigation. Don't go into this exercise with your magnifying glass and

CHAPTER THREE: THE APPROACH

voice recorder. If you trust me and set aside your protections, you will begin to feel freedoms in life that you have probably never experienced. I remember when I first started working with my current therapist. For about seven months, I would go to the lab every Tuesday, and she would have one assignment for me.

She would say, "Walter, you are going to have to allow yourself to be vulnerable. You will not be able to experience love or truly embrace who you are until you allow yourself the ability to be emotionally vulnerable and emotionally available."

To me, that sounded like the craziest thing in the world. Why would I give myself up emotionally and, on top of that, be vulnerable? I think you already know what my reply was; "Why would I give someone else the ability to control my emotions? Do people actually do that? I am not going to give someone the ability to make me unhappy or sad. I'm not giving in to anything or anybody. I'm an actor, so I can perform like I'm emotionally vulnerable." I would tell her I performed in both my marriages and they tried to take advantage of my feelings and emotions. "There's no way I'm going to freely give them to somebody!" And this would be my closer: "I can't even swim because you have to give yourself up to the water, and I'm not giving control to anything or anybody!"

Needless to say, it was coming pretty close to us mutually shutting down the lab I had with her. But one day I woke up and said, "Why not try it? She hasn't steered me wrong yet, and if I'm going to become the best version of myself, the reason I'm in therapy in the first place, I am going to have to challenge myself, anyway. So why not just jump off the deep end?" So that's what I did, and that has been the greatest decision I have made in my entire life. Why? Because I am genuinely being who I want to be.

I'm living a life of freedom. I'm no longer guarding myself from the idea that there may be pain or hurt attached to it, and to tell you the truth, it's a lot better on this side. Being protected and guarded, I lived so much of my

CHAPTER THREE: THE APPROACH

life trying to avoid the traumas and their triggers to create my own safe spaces. This really only left me with emptiness, and in a lot of cases, operating in transactional relationships because there was no trust here, there, or anywhere. When I tested being emotionally available and emotionally vulnerable, I realized I had taken my true relational power back, and it has given me confidence and changed my life. Your next questions probably are, "How did you do it, Walt?" and, "Walt, what does that look like?"

To answer your question about how I did it, I took baby steps. The first time I felt I allowed myself to be vulnerable was in a situation I had with my father. At the time, we had not spoken for about seven years. This was an issue I had been discussing in the lab with my therapist as well. I told my therapist I was going to reach out to my father to have a very open and honest conversation with him. Well, my plan was to have an open and honest conversation, but the honest part was to really explain and let him know how I truly felt. Not in a mean way, but in a truthful, yet vulnerable way. My assignment was to express my true feelings, but this time, I didn't want to take center stage and perform. It wasn't about protecting myself from getting hurt. For the first time in my life, I was going to allow myself (as I was thinking) the freedom to be unprotected and possibly knowingly walk myself right into hurt. Unbeknownst of my decision to speak to my dad after many years of silence, my little brother asked me to attend my father's birthday celebration, and I said, "Yes, I will come." I stood on my word and went. My brother felt like he had cured cancer, but we didn't have the talk that day. I felt it was the wrong time, wrong place. The following week is when I took him out to lunch, and we sat down to talk. I explained to him why we stopped talking (which he really didn't know), and I also shared the reason behind the action. What struck me though, **was how it made me feel emotionally**. It was in this conversation that I understood why vulnerability was important. The moment I became open and exposed in the conversation, it allowed him to react in a more open and transparent way. And secondly, it allowed us both to let our guards down and simply be unprotected together. To this day, our conversations no longer need to be guarded from one another, as they had been for the previous 40 years. I quickly found that the ability to be vulnerable could open up the pathway to healing and improving our mental health.

One of our friends, the Golden Dragon, attributes is self-discovery. What you will self-discover for yourself is vulnerability — it's where you can gain a more profound understanding of your emotions, motivations, and limitations. It is here that you allow yourself to face challenges head-on, learn from your setbacks, and develop the capacity to bounce back from your adversity. What I have found is that, even though it sounds counterintuitive, taking the risk of sharing our vulnerabilities can build self-confidence by realizing the capacity of our courage and resilience. In the upcoming chapters, I will delve deeper into the benefits of being emotionally vulnerable throughout this process. I hope this brief explanation gives you the courage and ability to step out and go through the exercise.

Exercise #1 is important because it is your first step in gaining confidence in your approach. By speaking to random people every day with your only intention being to brighten that moment in their day, will undoubtedly help you build your internal confidence. That when you speak with the right tone and presence, people will be more eager and happier to engage with you. Remember, the more consistent you are with your good mornings (and tweaking it for more positive results), the more confident you become in approaching the person or people you want to pursue. I still utilize this exercise, especially when I start to feel like I am losing my aura and comfort to make the initial approach. Because if making the initial approach is not natural for you, it can become easy to lose the new confidence you found if you are not steadily using the tools. So besides being nice and lifting people's day, this is a great way to keep your energy and confidence sharpened.

After about two weeks of practicing **Exercise #1**, you'll feel ready to start the total approach process. Some of you may have already gained enough confidence after a week and are approaching women with ease. I recommend finishing the book to have all your tools in your toolbox. However, if you need to start shooting your shot now, I can give you some foolproof pointers to get you started on your journey.

Exercise #2
FIRST, CHECK YOUR ENERGY LEVEL:

The first thing a woman notices about you, is your energy. With **Exercise #1**, you probably quickly found out that the more positive and joyful energy you brought, the more receptive they were to receive your good mornings. You have to understand that women have been getting hit on since they were teens, and a lot of times, it wasn't a pleasant experience for them. As we discussed earlier, the same way our traumas and triggers shape us, women have trauma and triggers when it comes to being approached. Have you ever been in the vicinity of a guy trying to shoot his shot (approach a woman)? He had the most hideous pickup line and when the woman doesn't accept his advancement, the man catches an attitude and says something negative about her or to her. It's situations like that, that she is preparing for every time a man walks up to shoot his shot. So, every time you approach a woman, you have to remember that scene in the back of your head. More than likely she is going to have that trigger ready when you show up. One way I know you can remove those triggers is in the way of your approach. Have positive, light, joyful energy. Your job is to alleviate all her initial guards. As she feels your approach is about to happen, she should feel it is going to be at least a positive experience. Just this act alone puts you ahead of most men when it comes to approaching women.

Exercise #3
CHECK YOUR POSTURE:

I have to be honest, I really didn't know how important this step was when it came to approaching women. A simple shoulder slump or the wrong head position — looking down or away instead of making eye contact — can

CHAPTER THREE: THE APPROACH

make or break an initial connection. If you are like me and have watched any of the wildlife shows, when it comes to a male preparing to approach his potential mate, no matter if it's a bird, lion, or gorilla, before he pursues, he checks his posture. They are all looking to be as appealing to her as possible. They stand with confidence. To catch her eye, they walk with a swag that says, "I am the only male for you." He gives off the energy that *I'm going to be your protector.* The males start giving off that *I'm big, I'm strong, I'm confident and I'm a keeper.* At the same time, he's showing her he is willing to be soft, loving, and safe for her. When they pan over to the female, if the posture is right for her, she is all into him even before any physical or verbal interaction he would make towards her. The animal kingdom has got it down. If you take notes from the animals and develop their natural instincts, you will be well on your way with your posture game. I must also add that you should feel like you are at your best because great posture is a feeling as well.

For reference, I recently went on a cruise, and before I got onboard, I was talking, chatting, and meeting people left and right. Then, when I got on the ship, I realized the majority of the cruise patrons were people in their 20s and early 30s, and the people around my age (50) were coupled up. By day two, I knew I wouldn't be making any love connections on the ship. I made the decision that I was just going to enjoy the experience for what it was going to be. I did just that. But by day four, I noticed my head wasn't up. I wasn't positively scoping the scenery. I noticed my shoulders went into more of a resting position, and my chest was not confidently taking the lead. I'm guessing that's why the people that I engaged with the first two days passed right by me the rest of the days; because my energy wasn't bringing fun, confident times. Our nonverbal communication speaks a lot louder than our audio communications. When it comes to approaching and engaging, believe me, your nonverbals oftentimes silence the verbal communication. So going back to the cruise, as soon as I stepped off the ship and into a new environment, away from the Gen Z'ers and young millennials, I felt a surge of positive energy, great posture. I returned to making positive approaches and engaging with others. So, make sure your posture is as positive as your energy. What energy am I talking about? I'm talking about a fresh haircut, brand-new outfit energy. Positive, confident, and joyful. Trust me, women definitely pick up on that.

Exercise #4
HOLD EYE CONTACT:

I used to have a bad habit of looking and freezing up as soon as I caught their eye. And I would probably do it about two to three times with them. I would look, they would look, then I would just as quickly turn my head like I wasn't just staring at them for the last 45 seconds. If you want to approach her, you cannot fumble this step. You can succeed in steps one and two, but if you fumble this step, it is all for not. It goes back to the basics, a woman wants a man who at least has enough confidence to hold eye contact with her. If you can't do that, how are you even going to have enough confidence to have a conversation with her? So please master these four steps as you prepare for the engagement process.

So, speaking of your approach.

Take the time to practice these four steps to approaching a woman. Set the tone by starting your days with affectious good morning energy. Check to ensure you are walking with positivity and confidence. Check your posture and practice holding eye contact. If you get comfortable or master all four steps, you will definitely have to rush to the next chapter to begin to work on your engagement.

CHAPTER FOUR
THE ENGAGEMENT

Engagement is what I call the art of first communication. Once you have done the work to approach her and prepare her for the initial engagement, the most important thing after that is how to break the ice. How do I open up? What do I do now? What should I say? Well, before we answer these questions, let me first give you my 4th chapter disclaimer, because I believe I need to.

When I began working on this chapter, I had to take a pause from writing and go to my lab for a consultation. I knew the title would stir up controversy. I'm in marketing, so I know how to market, but I didn't want the content to really be controversial. But as soon as I finished writing the outline, I was like, "Oh, this may be bad." I wanted to write this chapter in a way that doesn't promote manipulation, but I do understand that the information in this chapter may step on the doorstep of it. However, I am trying my hardest not to knock on the door. The reason I'm careful about how I lay out this information is not only because I'm a girl dad, but also because I'm writing this as a self-help book. My goal is to help you succeed — not to take advantage of women. So, let's delve in.

Well, let's first deal with what you should or shouldn't say. We all have our go-to lines or ways to start engagement. Even with those in mind, starting a conversation can still be one of the hardest things to do—mostly because we're guessing or just hoping that our line opens the door for further connection. Let's go over some common ones. For some people, they work, for others, not so much.

Let's see why they may or may not work for you:

What's up with you?

CHAPTER FOUR: THE ENGAGEMENT

Too abrasive, too direct

Yo, Baby/Yo, come here!
Anything with Yo, kill it.
It's also too intimate for strangers

If you look good now, I can only imagine you being made up.
This draws her intrigue

How are you doing?
Boring, not interesting

I appreciate a real woman.
It's subtle, draws her in

Hello, beautiful.   **NO!!** Let me explain

Hello, gorgeous.   **NO!!** Let me explain

    Okay, I know I have you perplexed now. The first five you get, but you're saying, and I can hear you, "But I can't call her beautiful, gorgeous, fine, or anything else that appreciates her overall beauty?" Yes, that is what I'm saying, and I have two great reasons why. First, she only really wants to hear that from two people in the world, and you can possibly only fit one of them, but it's not a guarantee. The only two people she wants to hear it from are her partner or someone she's crushing on and wants him to pursue her. Those are the only two people she wants to hear it from or, better yet, values it from. Everybody else, it may be appreciated, but it's not holding the value you think it is.

Secondly, after the "You are so beautiful" comment, there's usually nowhere else to go with the conversation. If she responds positively, you'll have to reinvent the dialogue because her only natural response is, "Thank you." "So, Walter, you're saying that I can't use those lines? Then what am I supposed to say or do?"

Well, I'm glad you asked. This is why I call it the art of engagement. I'm going to be very clear; I AM NOT GOING TO GIVE YOU MY GO-TO LINES (I may still have them in use). So, this is how successful engagement works.

CHAPTER FOUR: THE ENGAGEMENT

Your job during the initial engagement is to remove any potential triggers connected to her past traumas or negative experiences. That sounds like a whole lot on your shoulder for someone you have never met before, but remember, this is not any woman; this is a woman you are interested in getting to know. This woman may possibly be your wife or the person you want to do the rest of your life with. This is where your vulnerabilities come into play.

From your energy and eye contact in the approach, to ensuring you allow her to drop her triggers and guards, understanding her possible past experiences, and becoming emotionally available in the words you speak. I usually start with a compliment, but not one they've heard a thousand times. For example, I may compliment her dimples. It is a subtle way to let her know I was detailed and intentional about our engagement. This one statement pretty much always drops their guard. Now, guess what? Unlike telling her she is so beautiful, and you're pretty much one and done, in this approach, you are left holding several follow-up statements and questions in your hand that you can go to after the initial engagement. You must remember that communication is a key part of the engagement process. Let me be more accurate, confident communication is the key to this process. So, you ask, what is confident communication or conversation? What does that even look like? Well, let me explain.

I have worked in marketing for over the past 20 years. When I started, I struggled with selling and introducing our products and services because I lacked a solid understanding of our offerings. So, I would go out and try to pitch what we had to offer. I was struggling to give services away; our clients didn't even have to purchase anything. But because I wasn't confident in what I was pitching, I couldn't relate our services to our customers. It wasn't until I refined my pitch and closing statement that I gained confidence in my offerings, and my clients began to reach out for the services and benefits we offered. This is the approach I want you to take when trying to appeal to her in your engagement conversation. To guarantee your success, I need you to prepare your **opening pitch, your offer, and your close.**

To start, we will go over your open pitch. You need to choose three areas to compliment her, or three opening lines. This is what I call building out a web.

Exercise #5
BUILDING A WEB:

I call this exercise *building* a web because that's essentially what you are doing. I didn't know I was doing this until someone in the lab told me, and I realized that's exactly what I was doing. I told you the lab is important. They help you see things you can't see for yourself. They are especially important to this process of meeting people, but really, your overall growth.

When I first realized I was building a web, I was on vacation with my best friends, and we were hanging out at the bar for about four hours. It seemed like every girl wanted to sit next to us (the majority were Black too), and I was sitting there and not moving because I was all for the engagement. That whole night, I used my three openers and my best friend quickly noticed. Regardless of the women's responses, I knew what I was going to say next. Based on their response, I knew where I was going with the whole conversation without necessarily leading the conversation. You never want to feel like you are taking over or leading the conversation. Women don't like men that talk about themselves all night. That night, I was pretty successful in my engagements. Not only did I draw all the women's interest that night, but there was also a lot of contact information being exchanged with me.

The next morning, my friend rushed to tell our other friend, "Dude, I just watched a master class. Walt was spinning his web all night. You can see how the conversation began — he had the same three openers and that's when he started spinning. Based on their responses, he pretty much knew what he was going to say. He had his response already queued up. It was

CHAPTER FOUR: THE ENGAGEMENT

happening so naturally. Once his web was spun to his liking, he would lead them right into it, and they'd just get caught."

I'm definitely not giving you those openers for your web because back then, I was not in my self-help era, I was more on my toxic/manipulation tip. I informed you in the beginning of the chapter that I am being very careful not to knock on the door of manipulation. But I will walk you through how to build your own web.

To build your web, you have to take your three openers, or compliments, whatever you choose to do, and build around them.

For example, let's go with the dimples:

Me: You know, I couldn't help but notice that you have some very nice dimples.

Her: Thank you
(I have now given her the ability to think about releasing her guards.)

Me: I'm not usually into dimples like that, but yours definitely caught my eye. I think it brings out a glow in you or something. I noticed it and got this positive energy or vibe from you, so I had to come over and say something.

Her: Aww, thank you, that's sweet.
(Once again, her guards are dropping, and now she knows I can form and present thoughts. So, I have the possibility to be a good conversationalist.)

Me: So, let me know if I'm talking too much, but do dimples like yours run in your family, or is yours just a one-off?
(I lead the conversation with two complimentary statements. Now that I have taken her guards down, I have given her the opportunity to inform me how welcoming she is toward my engagement.)

Her: Oh, no, you're okay...

(That's what I wanted to hear. She just let me know she's comfortable with the engagement and would like to continue with the conversation. If you notice, I didn't give the second part of the answer

CHAPTER FOUR: THE ENGAGEMENT

to the question because since she has welcomed my interaction with her, I'm free to change subjects and can continue with an exploratory conversation. I will go more into how to have an exploratory conversation later. Now I switch the conversation into, "How's your day going?" "How are you enjoying the event?" "Are you from the area?")

Notice that the first five interactions are all scripted. The first two are just to get her to drop her guards, triggers, and tension. When approaching her, your main objective should be to alleviate any tension she has about being approached. Personally, intentional compliments work for me, but if you prefer opening lines, make sure they are light, positive, and engaging.

Let's try one for example:

Me: I really appreciate a real woman.

Her: Oh, thank you.

Me: I had to come over and say something. It's

not often now-a-days you find women confident enough to just be in their God-given beauty. Nothing fake, no makeup, just lipstick. That's what's up.

Her: Thank you. You noticed all that, that quick?

Me: I'm telling you it's rare, so yep, I noticed it that quick. But I was spot on, right? Just lipstick?

Her: Yes, I'm impressed.

Me: Well, I'm glad I was able to impress you and put a smile on your face. So, besides your current smile that I have to attribute to myself, how is your day going?

As you can see, this interaction went very well. She was asking questions before I could even get to mine. In this interaction, you could say my second comment released her triggers and dropped her guards. Just remember you want to feel like you are releasing her triggers and tension when you are giving your opening statements. Your goal is to ensure she is not uncomfortable with your approach.

Exercise #6
OPENING CONVERSATION ZONES:

I suggest you set up what I call conversation zones. I call them zones because just like a zone in football (either one), hockey, and basketball, you zone the conversation to your advantage. No matter what is said, you already have your response pretty much in place and you already know how you are going to follow up. Let's explore what they look like.

These are the basic zones you should have in place: **2-1-1, 2-2-1, 2-3**, or **3-2 zones**. This is essential to the web you are building.

A **2-1-1** is two compliments or openers, followed by one question, and the 1 represents that your third question is open-ended, which may lead her to ask you a follow-up question.

A 2-2-1 is two compliments or openers,

followed by two questions, and the 1 represents that your third question is open-ended, which may lead her to ask you a follow-up question.

A **2-3 zone** is two compliments or openers, followed by 3 questions she can only reply to.

A **3-2 zone** is three compliments or openers, followed by 2 questions she can only reply to.

You want to have these three combinations in place for all your lead compliments or openers. Because it depends on how the first two openers go, it will determine where you want to go with the conversation. You want to have a good feeling that her guards are down before you ask a question, and I suggest the first question should be in reference to the opener. Before you start asking questions, you should have a sense or idea if you have provided a safe space for her, and she feels comfortable with your engagement. To establish a dialogue, remember when delivering the first question, you are looking to see if she is willing to engage with you:

Is she giving you eye contact?
Is she smiling?
Is her posture appealing?
Does she seem to be open to more interaction?

These are some of the signs you are looking for as you are preparing to ask your first question. When you see any of these signs, you know you have dropped her guards, and you have made her feel safe in your interaction with her. Sometimes you might need to add another statement before a question, and that's the 3-2 zone. Here is an example of the 3-2 zone:

Me: You know, I couldn't help but notice, you have some very nice dimples.

Her: You think so?
(She definitely has her guards up, and who knows where she thinks this may go.)

Me: I definitely think so. I really don't even notice dimples, but yours certainly caught my eye.

Her: They caught your eye, huh?

(She has some intrigue but still has her guards up. But she is willing to give me a chance to make her feel safe.)

Me: Once I saw it, it was like a glow that hit me. Your dimples have a whole positive aura and energy attached to it. That's why I had to come over here and say something to you. Let's keep it real, saying you have nice dimples is the worst come-on line ever.

Her: *(She smiles or laughs.)*

(She may not have her guards down, but I have made her feel safe. Now I can ask a question.)

Me: Let me know if I'm talking too much, but do dimples like yours run in your family, or are yours just a one-off?

Her: My mom and brother have dimples, but I don't know if they glow or anything.

CHAPTER FOUR: THE ENGAGEMENT

(She didn't let me know she was comfortable with continual engagement, but she is giving me a space to communicate with her for the moment. Now I am free to ask a question, how do I know that? Her first response was a question back to me. Her second response was a gesture, she laughed. This last response, she opened up to me, letting me know about her family, then finished with a statement that didn't cut off communication. So, I can follow up with another question, but because her guards are not all the way down, I still need to go back to a comment before for the next question.)

Me: So, I guess you're a one-off. But seriously, you never heard that about your dimples?

(I just gave her the ability to show me if she is interested in further engagement. If she gives me a quick, "Nope." I know it's time to wind down my engagement, but more than likely at this point she is ready to engage and will respond as such.)

We have explored two of my suggested opening conversation zones. I didn't go over the perfect 2-1-1 zone or the 2-3 zone, but I hope you can get the gist of how to use it. What I want you to see and take away from these examples I just gave is that I started with the same opener. But I reacted to the responses I was given, and I did it with confidence because it was already prepared in my queue. If you have all your opening statements and questions in your zones, you are really never caught off guard at this crucial stage of engagement. Make sure that when you are creating your zones, you are doing them with this process in mind. You are walking up expecting to have a 2-1-1 experience, but if it's a 3-2 or a 2-3 experience, you will be well prepared for it.

Now after the fourth or fifth interaction, you are going to have a feeling if she is interested in furthering the conversation. If she is not, gracefully bow out with a, "I just had to let you know. You have a good day." But if she is interested in further engagement, it's time to start working on **Your Offer**.

I'm telling you, this is not what you expect it to be when I say *your offer*. This is not

CHAPTER FOUR: THE ENGAGEMENT

the place where you show her all you can do for her, and what you have to present to her. This is where you offer intention to her and an engaging ear. In marketing, after you give your client the reason you are there and have made them comfortable with your presence, your next goal, especially if you are not trying to make a quick sale or hustle something down their throat, is to give them space to tell their story. It is in their story you receive nuggets to further the dialogue and get an understanding to secure a sale and possibly a long-term relationship.

Probably like yourself, most people want to find or have a place safe enough to have conversation and communication. If this was not true, there would be no need to read this book or even pursue relationships in general. Your previous five interactions let you know she is okay with your communication. Now you just have to know where to take it and how to let her feel comfortable to where she knows she is free to openly engage with you. This is accomplished by how you present your question in your offer. Your offer questions should be about her but nothing direct or assertive. You want to also make sure you have some pivot questions. Pivot questions are questions that smoothly get you out of your zone questions. Here are some examples of pivot questions:

So, are you from this area?

So, besides me bothering you, how is your day going?

I see you have energy beads on. Do you know their healing properties?

That scorpion on your neck, does that signify you are poisonous and toxic, or are you just a Scorpio?

All these questions are light conversation starters, because you still want her to remain in her safe comfortable space. However, when you pivot your conversation, you always want her response to lead back to you. When you ask, "Are you from this area?" You have an 80% chance of getting a "Yes." Or "No." Followed by,

CHAPTER FOUR: THE ENGAGEMENT

"How about yourself?" That, *how about yourself*, puts the ball back in your court, and that's when you can go off and run with the conversation. Asking about the Scorpio, there is a 90% chance it's her astrology sign. Can you guess what she is going to ask you after that? Well, if you don't know, let me tell you. She is going to respond by saying, "What sign are you?" If you have pivot questions that you have a 70% or greater chance of knowing their response, why wouldn't you already have your own preset responses in your queue? Your job is to stay confident, and not flustered or awkward. The more prepared you are, the easier it is to communicate.

Previously in this chapter I talked about exploratory communication. I think now is a good space to delve into it. Exploratory communication is exactly what it sounds like. You're going on an exploratory expedition to see what she is about. Her interests, her likes, her possible concerns, and if the space and time is right, *her crazy*. Believe me, if you're going to ever get her own truth about her craziness, it's this (if you have the time), or the next two conversations. If you wait past the third conversation, she is probably actually starting to like you, and she is not going to be as open with that information. If you can get it out of her in the first three conversations, you will get the unadulterated truth of what you can expect to deal with at her worst.

When you move past your pivot and into exploration, you should start to gauge how much time you have to explore. What setting are you in? Did you meet in passing? How long will you be in the same space together? Does she have to connect with someone else after your engagement? All of this information is valuable when deciding where to go with your exploration, and what you want to get out of it. Believe me, women like exploratory conversation because they feel like you have a genuine interest in them and what she is about. Here is how exploration conversations work. When seeking information, you want to be transparent and open about yourself to lead her to be open about herself. So here is an example of moving from a pivot to an exploration conversation:

Her: Definitely not toxic, But yes, I'm a Scorpio. What is your sign?

Me: How do you know I would even know what my sign is?

Her: Because you are being nosey and asking me about mine.

(She is jovial, her guards are dropping, and she is comfortable with banter.)

Me: Well since you want to follow my noseiness, and be nosey yourself, I'm a Pisces. A February Pisces. Do you know anything about them? Are you into Astrology or Tarot or anything like that?

(She is more than likely going to tell me her religious faith.)

Her: I'm not into it all like that, I just know my birthday is November 13th and that's Scorpio season.

(Awe, she didn't tell me her faith.)

Me: You don't know it at all like that. You must be a good church girl? I'm a preacher's kid myself, so I know all about not following astrology, tarot, palm reading, and lighting candles and things.

(Here's my second attempt.)

Her: I'm a Christian but I'm not in church like every Sunday, I just never got into astrology like that.

(Okay, I just got her religion.)

Me: I heard that, you must be a heathen like me?

Her: I'm not going to call myself a heathen, I just don't be at church every Sunday.

Me: So, what do you do on Sunday? Do you go to festivals, brunches or concerts?

CHAPTER FOUR: THE ENGAGEMENT

(I'm about to find out what she likes to do.)

Her: I do go to church, but not every Sunday. You have me over here feeling like the biggest sinner right now for missing a couple of Sundays. But I do like to go to festivals, concerts, comedy shows, and things like that. But I also like hiking, camping, and fishing.

(She just told me what she likes to do for fun.)

I hope you see what I just did and achieved. In a light non-intrusive conversation, I found out she is really not into astrology, she is a Christian, and what she likes to do. Also, remember if you can, and you believe time permits, draw out your replies to her for about 3-6 minutes on your end, and make sure it always leads back to her. This will do two things for you: first, it would let her know you have great communications skills, which women yearn for. But most importantly, I have noticed when I stop talking, I'm focused on hearing what she has to say in return because I'm going to have to create another 3-5 minutes of conversation from what she says. This will definitely improve your listening skills and your memory. This really works to my advantage, and I can guarantee it will work to your advantage as well. I understand if you're not a good talker or communicator, but if you have some exploratory questions in your queue, it will become that much easier as you gain confidence in your material.

We have been going over a lot, and it's time to prepare for the close. To achieve high success in your approach and engagement, you must have a strong close. In the next chapter, we will focus on the close, so let's get started.

CHAPTER FIVE
THE CLOSE

———◆—•◆•—————◆———

Before we begin to focus on our close, let's go back to our friend, the Golden Dragon. As a recap, our friend is often said to emerge from chaos, bringing order. It is also believed that the connection to our friend leads to the development of inner strength and self-discovery. Throughout the course of this book, we have embarked on a self-discovery and self-healing journey to understand where you lack confidence and the ability to approach and engage confidently with the women you would like to pursue.

Through your own personal self-reflection and the tools we have discussed in this book, you should find yourself more confident in your ability to approach and engage. You now have a pretty strong roadmap for successful engagement. One more thing before we get into the close. I want to bring up one very important piece of information for your success. The tools I have given you are almost foolproof to open the doors to conversation and engagement. One thing I want to be very clear about is this: you have to know what you are attracted to. More importantly, you need to know who you are attracted to and what they typically require.

    I will not start painting pictures of the visual aspect of a woman, so I will just say this, if you have a propensity or an attraction for women that may be looking for nothing more than a transactional relationship over a true partnership to build with each other, then when you are ready to step to her with your approach, make sure you are looking the part as well. If you are attracted to women who love to travel, but on your dime, or they love to eat at high-end restaurants, but only on your dime, make sure when you are getting ready for your approach, you present yourself in a way that gives off the

CHAPTER FIVE: THE CLOSE

impression that you can provide that lifestyle. The methods in this book will still help you reach the second or third compliment. But there's less chance of success if you don't appear to be able to provide the lifestyle she's looking for, or to be successful when you reach the questions stage. So that's just a reminder and a tip for you.

Let's get to the closing. This is why you approached her in the first place. It's time to explore how to close the engagement with her. I wanted to make "the close" its own chapter because it's that important. Many businesses don't succeed not because their product is bad or because they do not know how to create good engagement with the customers. Many businesses fail because the owner and their team did not know how to close the deal. They are great at getting people to look at their product, and even better at having people to engage with it; however, when it comes to closing the deal, they lack a clear understanding of how to do it. So, they end up going out of business. Throughout this book, you may notice that I have treated you as a commodity or a product.

I have spent the time showing you your value, and after a few tweaks, why you are worthy.

I have identified some of the best ways to get in front of and engage with your potential partner. More than likely, by this point, you have probably gone through some or all of the exercises. You have found out they work, and you are probably getting comfortable with them. You have even possibly started approaching and engaging with women and found success there. If you are him, I want to offer congratulations for working on your own inner confidence, stepping out of your fears and protections, and allowing yourself to be vulnerable and courageous in pursuing what you desire.

Exercise #7
THE CLOSE:

Once again, the close is not your final sales pitch. A lot of people, especially the used car salesmen type, or the hustling type, sell at the opening pitch, their offer, and their close. If you haven't convinced them of the value in the opening pitch or the offer, it is highly unlikely that you will convince them in your close. The close is not for you to sell or convince; the close is for you to gauge her interest and create and finalize your offer.

So how do you gauge a woman's interest? Is it by her facial features? Her gestures? Her posture? I would say, "Yes." All of them play a part in evaluating her interest, and you should be looking for positive signs in those areas. Nevertheless, the sure-fire way to gauge her interest is with some questions, and please DON'T blurt out, "Are you interested in me?" That's definitely not the question you want to ask. I will say never ask that question, but especially not at this point. "So, Walt, what are some good closing questions I can ask?" Yes, I heard you just ask me that question. Let's explore some options.

As you may have noticed in my opening pitch or offer, I never asked for her name. Some people start there. Her tension and guards are still up when they ask her this question, so they might get her name, but they are losing the value of this question by putting it at the beginning instead of at the close. If you ask her name in the close, you can undoubtedly gauge her interest. For instance:

Me: So, by the way, may I ask for your name?

Her: Michelle, and what's yours?

(She extends her hand out for a handshake.)

From this interaction, I have gauged that she has drawn interest, has appreciated the interaction we have had thus far, and is open to more. How did I gauge that? After she gave me her name, she asked for mine. That was number one. She showed interest in wanting to learn more about me. Secondly, the thing I gauged was that she reached out for a handshake. This shows me that it's her subtle way of providing a bid for connection. If I started off by asking her name and she did those two exact things, at best, you can take it that she's being cordial. Let's review some other closings:

CHAPTER FIVE: THE CLOSE

1.   I like your vibe. Do you have any space in the upcoming days for future conversations?

2.   It was a pleasure talking to you, but I just had to tell you about… (whatever the compliment was about.)

3.   I know you have to go, but can I ask you…

I'll give you one more because, honestly, you will be coming up with your own as you create your own web and flow. These are just examples.

4.   It was great chatting with you. I hope I haven't slowed down your day.

If you look at these opening closers, besides number one, where you feel you have an excellent chance in this connection, they are all questions to gauge where she is with your engagement. If you get positive energy from these questions, it's time to ask for contact information. If you are still hesitant, you can ask if they have social media accounts and choose which one you would like to share with each other. For me, I bypass social media and go straight for the phone number. If I have the phone number, I have direct access to either text or call her. No longer do I have to gauge our engagements to see if she is feeling me or not. I then have control of the engagement I want to have with her, and my initial pursuit is done.

So here are some follow-up closing questions to "close the deal":

1.   I don't want to hold up too much of your time. Are you on social media?

2.   I need to get going. It was a pleasure talking to you. I would love to chat with you some more. Do you mind exchanging numbers?

3.   I like this energy we have. Let's exchange numbers.

CHAPTER FIVE: THE CLOSE

All of these methods are sure-fire ways to close the engagement and get the results you want.

As I close out this book, I want to review a couple of key points with you. Generally, the hardest thing for many men to do is approach a woman. A man doesn't know what is on the other side of his approach. When he gets ready and makes the decision to approach a woman, he often gets butterflies in his stomach. He gets extremely nervous. The fear of instant rejection brings heat to his body as he is about to open his mouth. Ladies who are still reading this book, it can be a daunting task for some men, I assure you. So, brotha's, that feeling I just described regarding us, a lot of the ladies experience the same feelings as they are being approached. So, in your approach, even before you say a word, you should be doing all you can to lower her tension and lower her guards.

Remember your posture. Is it threatening? Remember your energy level. Is it positive and non-aggressive? Is your eye contact producing cheerful interaction? These are things you can always work on and tweak to fit you.

Now when it comes to your engagement, this is the area that can really put fear in us like no other. I suggest that you take some time to address the pains and hurts from your past and youth that have contributed to your loss of confidence in the first place. When you truly feel your best, you will unquestionably operate at your best. The tools I have laid out in the book will work, even without self-evaluation and self-work. But doing the work of removing all the lies of your past and really knowing that your value and worth are not based on others' preferences will put you in such a positive and confident place that approaching and engaging with women you want to pursue, it will become seamless to you.

Now as I close this book out, once again I want to refer to the Golden Dragon. The Golden Dragon signifies transformation and spiritual enlightenment. It's often seen as a guardian, offering guidance through trials and

CHAPTER FIVE: THE CLOSE

tribulations. Its majestic presence serves as a powerful reminder of personal potential. It was at the Golden Dragon I was given the opportunity to receive the spiritual enlightenment that would change my life, and like another one of his attributes, the dragon doesn't hoard its treasures. Instead, the dragon is known to share them, bringing prosperity to those who are worthy and pure of heart. So, this is my attempt to share with others the lessons I learned from my own personal struggles, failures, and successes trying to navigate the dating world. In hopes that you may find nuggets from my success and create your own. It will be my greatest wish that when you find your own success, do not hoard it, but do the same and spread it with others.

ACKNOWLEDGEMENTS

Thank you to all my children, biological and acquired; you all have been my motivation to push myself to places and spaces I never dreamed of getting to or accomplishing in this life. You guys have changed my mindset from trying to be the richest and most successful person around to focusing on the legacy I leave on this earth, and this book is a part of it.

I want to thank my Lab, my best friends Linze and Donald, who are just always a phone call away. When I was going through my separation and ending to my marriage, Linze called every morning on our way to work — which is now our four years running morning routine — and never talked about my situation unless I brought it up, and boy, was that needed during that time. Donald, my voice of reason through all my shenanigans during my space-filling days. "That Boy needs help." And "What are we going to do with Walt?" Will always rings through my ears."

Also in my Lab is my spiritual adviser, Dr. Sir Winston. Whenever I need spiritual wisdom, he is always there to give it in a loving way. But he has definitely not been my "Yes Man". Your guidance and understanding have truly helped me get to the place I am today.

Some or most may say, "My favorite cousin." Chanee, thank you for being my go-to for everything, woman. Even though we've had our share of toxicity report sessions, when it comes to advice on this book and woman, you were always there and spot on.

One of the reasons this book is written is because of my cousin KaRon. I thank you for always having my back from our toddler years, and I'm especially grateful to you for getting me to go out that faithful night to the Golden Dragon.

I cannot forget my therapist that I have continued to rock with over the past four years. I won't give your name, but you have not only saved my life but have given me a greater appreciation and understanding for the life I live.

My acknowledgements wouldn't be complete without my dear friend Keisha, who was the one I went to when I was writing and not trying to be manipulative in my writing. Her clinical background in Speech Language Pathology and the way she helped me guide my writing was almost as valuable as our friendship.
Then there is Revision Publishing, which wasn't in my lab before this book but has definitely found a space in it now. The meetings, the work, and the pushing to perfection were just what I needed, so thank you and welcome to the Lab.

I want to thank my parents for the guidance you provided me as a child, young adult, and man, helping me reach this point in time.

Last but not least, I want to acknowledge you. I would like to thank the person who picked up or opened the book at the bookstore, the person who bought the eBook, and the person who bought the audiobook. I hope you get everything and more than you expect from this book.

BLACK GIRL UGLY

The Art of Approach and Engagement

www.ingramcontent.com/pod-product-compliance
Lightning Source LLC
Chambersburg PA
CBHW052032030426
42337CB00027B/4978